Hartmut Wilke

Turtles

**How to Take Care of Them and
Understand Them**

Expert advice on environmental
needs of the species

With 40 color photographs;
drawings by Karin Heckel-Merz

Consulting Editor:
Matthew M. Vriends, PhD

BARRON'S

Contents

Preface

Turtles can live to be very old in human care. Unfortunately, however, turtles owners often enjoy their pets for only a brief time. Research has shown that over 80 percent of turtles die in the first year. Such sad results—usually caused by a lack of information—can be avoided by learning how to take care of a turtle in a way appropriate to the species.

In this Barron's Pet Owners Manual, the author, Hartmut Wilke, explains what is essential in the appropriate care of land, water, and marsh turtles. On how-to pages accompanied by graphic illustrations, the author gives precise instructions for proper housing in a terrarium or aquarium. In addition, he offers advice—well-tested in practice—on appropriate feeding and on hibernation, which is so important for turtles' well-being.

This book supplies essential information on a topic of vital importance in keeping turtles: species conservation. Protected species are clearly marked in the individual instructions on taking care of popular species of turtles. Authoritative advice, easily understandable instructions, fascinating color photographs, and informative drawings make this book an indispensable guide for all those who keep turtles.

The author and the editors of Barron's Pet Owners Manuals wish you great pleasure with your turtle.

Caring for turtles brings peace and tranquility into everyday life. This will last, however, only if you are prepared to invest time and money in order to meet the turtles' changing needs.

Please see the Important Information on page 63.

Advice on Making Your Purchase

Don't confuse technical perfection and the investment of capital with loving care. In the final analysis, it alone is crucial for the turtle's well-being. And it is possible only if you intensively gather information about the turtle's biology and necessities of life.

For over ten years I have been advising turtle owners, and in so doing have made the acquaintance of likable, amusing people. In every case, they were eager to do only what was best for their shelled pets. But most of them see me only when they are deeply disappointed, with pets that are often near death. This is especially traumatic for children and adolescents, who cling to their "Felix" or "Susi" with enthusiasm and devotion. I am saddened too, because each time I am an unwilling witness to the increase in the number of unsuccessful attempts to keep a turtle. Yet it is not so very difficult to make the turtle a companion that its owner may enjoy from childhood on—until he or she is well advanced in years. Therefore, while reading this book, consider whether you can meet the requirements for doing so.

Ten Aids to Reaching a Decision

1. With good care, turtles easily can reach an age of 60 years and more. Keep this in mind when buying your turtle.

2. Many species require a winter rest period for their well-being, and many even need a summer rest period.

3. Is it possible for you to offer your turtle an outdoor enclosure in the yard in summer? Fresh air and sun are good for it.

4. The terrariums needed are usually larger than imagined—and the price increases along with the size!

5. Terrariums for marsh and water turtles must be watertight. Nevertheless, the floor beneath them ought to be able to withstand an occasional slosh of water.

6. Large aquariums for water turtles are heavy. A medium-sized basin with 52 gallons (200 L) of water, a stand, and accessories easily weighs 551 pounds (250 kg). Will your floor bear that?

7. Many turtles are active at twilight or at night. During the day they sleep in a hiding place.

8. Turtles are wild animals and remain so even if they are reproduced in captivity. They are not suited to be cuddly pets.

9. Providing food is not always simple. Even commercially prepared food has to be supplemented with fresh food.

10. Turtles don't like to go on trips. Do you have someone available to take care of your pet when you're on vacation?

Should You Keep One Turtle or Two?

Although you may have seen pictures of large "turtle congregations" in nature, turtles are loners. True, they are found in large numbers in favorite sunny spots or in rich pasture lands, but, unlike humans, they are not de-

A European pond turtle (left) and a Caspian turtle (right) sunbathing.

pendent on a social life. They can manage very well on their own. Only if you wish to breed turtles will you need to purchase a pair. In so doing, always remember that room will be needed later for the young as well (see page 39).

Taking care of several turtles involves a risk for the beginner, particularly if the turtles are kept in too small a space. Often females are continually attacked and bitten by males eager to mate. For the female this frequently leads to serious injuries, lingering illness, and death. A female in this kind of predicament must be able to get to a place safe from the male.

Competitive struggles between two males, when a female is present as a third party, have exactly the same consequences. Be careful also with water turtles of different sizes. As a rule, they pounce ravenously on their food, which always has to float in the water. As a result, the head of a very small turtle can easily get between the sharp jaws of a large one if they both snap at the same piece of food.

Every turtle would like to have a hiding place where it can feel safe.

Male or Female?

If you're looking for a suitable mate for your turtle, you will have to choose from nearly full-grown animals. The younger the turtle, the more difficult it is to distinguish between the sexes. In the males of many species the abdominal shell, or plastron, is curved inward more deeply than that of the females (see illustration, page 7).

Males, as a rule, also possess a somewhat longer tail, narrower at its base, and the cloaca is located closer to the tip of the tail. This can be determined, however, only in a direct comparison of several animals of approximately the same size. Half-grown male painted turtles can be recognized quite clearly by the front claws, which are plainly longer than those of the females.

How Old Is the Turtle?

If you don't know the turtle's year of birth, you will have to rely on estimates. After three years the animal attains about one-third of its final size (see Popular Turtle Species, page 50); after three more years it reaches two-thirds of its final size. This is a fairly rough indication, because the growth rate depends very heavily on the living conditions. The rate of growth slows down increasingly with age.

It is not true that age can be read by the "annual rings" on the plates, or scutes, of the dorsal shell, or carapace.

Where Can You Get Turtles?

In pet stores you will usually find species that are not protected. Protected species with a CITES (Washington Convention on International Trade in Endangered Species of Wild Fauna and Flora) certificate (see page 7) are, as a rule, more likely to be obtained from a breeder as young animals. I would like to advise, however, against purchasing a turtle by mailorder. You cannot determine a turtle's state of health until you personally have seen the animal.

Often a land turtle or tortoise succeeds in rolling over out of the dorsal position only after a long struggle.

Is the Turtle Healthy?

When examining a turtle to determine the state of its health, consider the following:
- Is the turtle's shell undamaged and firm? It should not give when pressed lightly between your fingers (see illustration, page 33).
- The animal's eyes must be open, clear, and bright.
- The areas around the nose and eyes should not be sticky with mucus (see symptoms, page 34).

What You Need to Know about Species Conservation

The Washington Convention on International Trade in Endangered Species (CITES) regulates the protection of species of fauna and flora that are endangered worldwide. According to the degree of their need for protection, most turtle species are placed in conservation categories I, II, and III. Animals that are threatened by extinction or that were classified as such by the commission on species conservation will be found in Appendix I of the CITES. For turtle species grouped in Appendix II and Appendix III, the regulators permit a controlled removal from their natural habitat.

Turtles threatened with extinction (CITES I species) may not be bought or sold, even if the animals have been produced through ranching. Trade in ranched animals of the especially protected species (all CITES II and III species), however, may be resumed.

The turtles offered in pet stores meet the legal requirements for species conservation and thus may be purchased legally. In so doing, keep in mind your own accountability.

Accountability: As the owner of a protected species of turtle, you must furnish proof of legal possession. The CITES certificate, being an identification card, meets these requirements. Without this official document you may not buy or sell a turtle (see page 39).

Obligation to inform the authorities: The owner of a protected species of turtle must report possession of the animal to the proper wildlife conservation authority without delay. The following information is required: species, age, sex, origin, habitat, intended purpose, distinguishing features, and registration number of the CITES certificate.

The female (above) and the male (below) are distinguished by different tail lengths.

Housing Turtles Properly

Through imaginative design and effective lighting you can create in terrariums lovely miniature landscapes that are a decorative feature in a room. The terrarium scenery, however, should not be changed continually: the turtle could no longer find its way around and would never feel quite at ease.

Please give attention to the varying living requirements of land, marsh, and water turtles. The design features and size of the terrariums are closely related to these requirements. The turtle always needs an enclosed area protected from drafts. Moving your turtle back and forth between a cardboard box and the floor, even if heated, will lead inevitably to the animal's early death.

My suggestion: If a turtle living in the wild has found a home with you and you don't know whether it is a land, marsh, or water turtle, you can classify it by looking at its feet. Water turtles, in contrast to land turtles, have webbing between their toes.

Useful Technical Accessories

You will need various technical accessories, depending on the type of terrarium used (see How-To for a Terrarium, pages 10–11; How-To for an Aquarium, pages 14–15). So that you don't miss any important information, here is a checklist to review:
- An electrical element with a thermostat for bottom heating.
- A spotlight and an ultraviolet lamp.
- A time switch to ensure a certain period of "sunlight" (see illustration, page 22).
- An outside filter for water turtles.

My suggestion: Use activated charcoal (which is quite expensive) as a filter mass only if you want to remove the yellowish color (the end products of protein metabolism) from the water. Charcoal is really not needed for any other purpose in keeping turtles. If you want clear water, it is cheaper to change it frequently.
- An air pump to circulate the water if no outside filter is available.
- An aquarium heater.
- A thermometer to measure the temperature of the air and water.

Important: Never place a pane of glass between the spotlight or ultraviolet lamp and the turtle; it might crack from the heat and filter the ultraviolet rays.

The Right Lighting

For terrariums housing land or marsh turtles, as well as for water turtles' aquariums, use a fluorescent lamp for general lighting in the daytime and a spotlight as a heat source from above. When raising young turtles, or when keeping your turtle outside in summer is not possible, you will need an ultraviolet lamp, placed about 3 feet (1 m) away. It should burn from 15 to 30 minutes at midday. A time switch makes turning it on and off more convenient.

Important: "Ultraviolet" should not be confused with "infrared" radiation! Ultraviolet lamps usually can be bought in a pet store.

In an outdoor terrarium the food is often more diversified than in one indoors.

Decorations

Decorating the terrarium turns out best when you are familiar with your turtle's natural biotope and its need for exercise. The animal should receive as many sense stimuli as possible: there must be obstacles in the form of rocks and branches to be walked around or climbed over. There should be nooks and crannies that invite turtles to look for food, to rest, or to hide.

Thick branches laid flat are inviting to a turtle that is a good climber. They must be wide enough for the animal to walk along them comfortably. If the terrarium has a strong bottom, you can also build rock terraces. It is advisable to keep the scenery of the terrarium as unchanged as possible throughout the animal's life span so that your pet has a perpetually familiar territory. Wilted plants or rotten branches may, of course, be removed.

How-To for Terrariums

1 Cork (1), three layers of aluminum foil (2) heating pad (3), clay floor tile (4), and air grate (5).

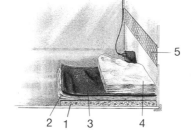

2 Mixture of sand and bark (1), clay water basin (2).

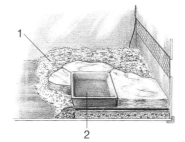

3 A fully equipped terrarium for land turtles. The glass cover (1) should cover only two-thirds of the terrarium. The lighting consists of a spotlight (2), an ultraviolet lamp (3), and a fluorescent lamp (4).

A Terrarium for Land Turtles and Tortoises

Land turtles want an "adventure playground" where they can poke about and climb around.

Terrarium size: Multiply the length of the **full-grown** turtle's shell by 5 for the length and width (surface area) of the terrarium. This measurement is applicable for turtles that are housed singly. For each additional turtle, increase the surface area by one-third.

Technical Assembly: Proceed as follows, working from bottom to top:

Figure 1

• Place a sheet of pressed cork between ⅕ and ⅘ of an inch (½–2 cm) thick and measuring about 12 by 16 inches (30 × 40 cm) in the turtle's future resting place (for heat insulation).

• Put down three layers of aluminum foil—all the same size as the cork sheet—with the reflecting side upward.

• Lay down an electric heating pad with a thermostat (available in pet stores), the same size as the foil and cork layers.

• Add a clay (terra cotta) floor tile or a concrete paving slab.

Figure 2

• Next to the slab place a water basin so that at least half of it is warmed by the heating pad. Most suitable for this purpose is a large clay flowerpot saucer that will comfortably accommodate the turtle even when fully grown. Your pet, however, should be able to climb over the side easily while it is still small.

• Now fill the remainder of the terrarium with a mixture of clean, very fine grained river sand and bark chips (mixed in a 1:1 ratio).

Figure 3

• Arrange the roots and rocks to create the desired "adventure playground" and a hiding place for nighttime.

A Terrarium for Marsh Turtles

Marsh turtles, like land turtles, need an "adventure playground" on land and, in addition, a "swimming pool," where they can swim and dive extensively. Therefore, a terrarium for marsh turtles should be watertight.

To house your marsh turtle, I recommend an aquarium that you can buy, build, or have built. Here, as well, a terrarium/aquarium that is as large as possible makes decorating easier.

Terrarium size: Calculate the size for a single turtle as described for land turtles.

Figure 1

Technical assembly: The terrarium corresponds to a large extent to that for land turtles. For the marsh turtle, however, note the following special features:

Figure 2

• Unlike the land turtle's terrarium, this one needs two thermostat-controlled heating pads underneath, one to warm the water and the other to warm the land portion (usually to a lesser extent).

• Fill the rest of the terrarium with a mixture of sand and bark chips, as described in detail for the terrarium to house land turtles.

My suggestion: Place a border of flagstones around the swimming basin, so that the water in the basin is not fouled so quickly by dirt that is carried in. These flagstones simultaneously can serve as the turtle's basking spot, warmed from below.

Figure 3

• The swimming basin should take up one-fourth to one-third of the area of

the aquarium, sloping gradually from the edge to a depth that corresponds approximately to twice the height of the full-grown turtle's shell. As a rule, a water depth of about 5 to 6 inches (12–16 cm) will suffice. A large clay dish in which you can lay flagstones as a "little staircase" makes a highly suitable water basin for marsh turtles.

1 A marsh turtle's terrarium with a large swimming basin. The ventilation grate (1) ensures good air circulation. The lighting, as in the case of the terrarium for land turtles consists of a fluorescent lamp, an ultraviolet lamp, and a spotlight.

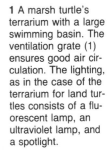

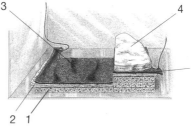

2 Cork (1), three layers of aluminum foil (2), two heating pads (3), and flagstone (4).

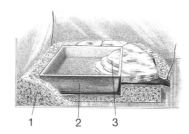

3 Sand and bark mixture (1), clay water basin (2), and flagstones (3) as a staircase.

The male has to get the female in the mood with courtship rituals.

Turtles are not necessarily dependent upon a partner. They can manage quite well on their own. If you are taking care of several turtles, make sure the terrarium is not too small, in order to prevent serious conflicts among the turtles.

Putting in Plants

Putting plants in the terrarium is not absolutely essential in providing for a turtle's needs. An attractively planted terrarium, however, helps create a harmonious impression overall and has an aesthetic appeal.

For turtle terrariums, only very robust plants are feasible; moreover, the turtles must be kept from eating them. The plants are best protected by a cylinder of tree bark (available in gardening supply stores) surrounding the root and stem areas.

A good exposure is of vital necessity for plants in a terrarium; without it they wither away. See that they are located in a well-lit spot, or light the plants with a special lamp that pet stores and gardening supply stores keep in stock for these purposes.

Dry terrariums for land turtles should be planted with the following: bromeliads such as *Guzmania,* species of *Aechmea,* and tall, robust plants such as *Yucca aloifolia, Schefflera, Sansevieria, Cordyline, Beaucarnea, Aspidistra,* and *Aloe.*

Marshy terrariums may be planted with the following: *Acorus, Aucuba, Chamaedorea, Ctenanthe, Cyperus, Dracaena,* and *Pittosporum.*

Aquariums are not planted with anything, because turtles "clear away" every visible piece of greenery. Try to compensate for the lack of decor in the basin by placing plants nearby.

ng the act of mating,   *the male often makes noises.*

Advice for taking care of plants and copiously illustrated descriptions will be found in various books on house and garden plants.

Where to Put the Terrarium or Aquarium

The location of a terrarium or aquarium in which turtles are kept must follow certain guidelines. There must be plenty of light, but the container should not stand all day in the blazing sun, because poorly ventilated terrariums get too hot. It should be in a quiet spot, not right next to a television set or stereo system. It should also be draft-free, a safe distance away from windows or terrace doors that are often open for ventilation.

The Quarantine Terrarium

A newly acquired turtle should be taken care of in a quarantine terrarium (see illustration, page 23) until you can be sure that your pet is indeed healthy (see Quarantine Is Indispensable, page 20). For this purpose, use a small version of the type of terrarium that you've chosen and equip it according to the directions on the How-To pages of this guide (pages 10–11 and 14–15). A quarantine terrarium, however, contains no decorations of any kind and is supplied only with a hiding place for the turtle. Everything must be easy to clean and disinfect thoroughly.

How-To for Aquariums

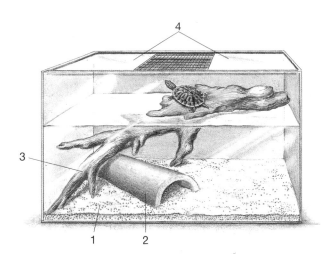

1 A simply equipped aquarium for water turtles. Clean sand (1), a piece of ridge tile (2), a branch of marsh pine (3), and a glass cover (4).

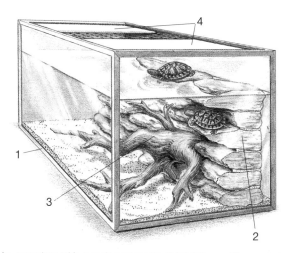

2 An aquarium with a rock wall made of fieldstones. The aquarium with its frame (1), stones used to form a rock wall (2), a branch of marsh pine (3), and a glass cover (4). A gap between the rock wall and the rear wall of the aquarium provides room for a heater and for ventilation.

An Aquarium for Water Turtles

Many water turtles are energetic swimmers. They want to have as much room as possible in which to swim. Therefore, the surface area as well as the water level of your aquarium are important. The only exceptions are a few turtle species such as the soft-shelled turtle, which spends its time at the bottom of the water (see Popular Turtle Species, page 50).

Calculate the size of an aquarium for a single animal roughly as follows: Multiply the length of the **full-grown** turtle's shell (see page 50) in inches times five to obtain the length of the aquarium; for the width, multiply the length of the shell by three.

The water should be at least roughly 1 foot (30 cm) deep. The measurements above apply to a "bare" aquarium, containing perhaps nothing more than a pine root and a few rocks as decoration. If you want to approximate nature more closely with a rock wall, roots, and a sandy bottom, the turtle will lose some of its swimming area. Offset this loss in advance by adding 30 percent to the figure you obtain for the aquarium's volume. An increase of the same amount is advantageous if you want to have a second turtle in the aquarium.

Technical Assembly: Assembling the aquarium is simple if you are satisfied with a minimum solution:

Figure 1

- A thin layer of clean sand covers the glass bottom so that it does not reflect.
- A piece of ridge tile on the bottom

serves as a hiding place, and a branch of marsh pine helps the turtle get its bearings.

Figure 2

- If you build a rock wall of flagstones on the rear wall of your aquarium, the result will be decorative in any room. A foam used in mounting or ready-mix cement will create a stronger bond betwen the stones. Leave a narrow crack of 1⅕ to 2 inches (3–5 cm) between the rocks and the rear wall. Later you will need to remove the dirt that builds up.

Important: The load-carrying capacity of aquarium bottoms is dependent on the strength of the glass. Your pet store dealer will tell you about its bearing power.

- An aquarium heater made of glass and equipped with a thermostat can be concealed easily behind the rock wall or attached with suction cups in a back corner. Protect the heater with a marsh pine root so that the turtle cannot damage the heating system. The wattage (capacity) of the heater depends on the quantity of water. Your local pet store dealer will advise you. To prevent broken glass use metal heaters or heaters housed in a filter.

Figure 3

- Resting places right below and on the water surface are also necessary. Fasten two cork sheets together with strong wire to form two platforms. Secure the resting place to a mount, for example, to the glass crosspiece of the aquarium.

4 The technical equipment for the aquarium. Glass container (1), an island for basking (2), an ultraviolet lamp (3), a spotlight as a source of heat (4), a fluorescent lamp (5), a heating pad with a styrofoam underlay (6), a thermostat with a sensing device (7), an air pump (8), an external filter (9), a glass cover (10).

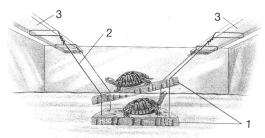

3 A floating cork island gives the turtles a place to bask. Cork sheets (1) wire (2), glass crosspiece (3).

Figure 4

- About three-fourths of the aquarium is protected from drafts by a glass cover. The "island" is suspended beneath the opening, while the spotlight and ultraviolet lamp hang above the opening.

- Next to or under the aquarium there is room for an air pump and filtering plant.

Important: The air pump and filter set up vibrations that must be prevented from reaching the aquarium. Put the equipment on a nearby table or wall bracket.

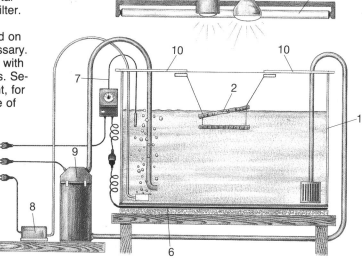

An outdoor pen can offer turtles a "dream vacation." Set aside a part of your yard for this purpose. If need be a corner of your balcony or roof garden will do, if it is protected from drafts.

The male red-eared turtle has very long claws.

Keeping Land Turtles and Tortoises Outdoors

Unless they are given Vitamin D, people forced to live without light and sunshine will develop serious bone diseases. Their legs and spine become deformed. This illness, called rickets, can be treated by exercise in the fresh air and sunshine.

Turtles, too—young ones in particular—fall ill if they lack light, sunshine, and vitamins. Their shell grows soft and becomes deformed. This explains the high cost for the equipment necessary to keep turtles indoors. In the long run, it is easier to keep them in an outdoor enclosure (see drawing, page 18) during the summer.

Size: Width, at least 4 feet (1.2 m); length, at least 9 feet 11 inches (3 m).

Enclosure: Cement tiles, lawn edging tiles, or smooth wooden planks set in the ground. Make sure the turtle cannot reach the upper edge of the enclosure with its front feet, so that it cannot climb out.

A young red-eared turtle in an outdoor pen.

Bottom of the fenced-in area: Dig down about 1 foot (30 cm); the ground should have a grade of about 2 inches (5 cm) for every 39 inches (1 m).

Plants: Sow grass and weeds on the bottom of the enclosure, and plant small bushes. Rocks and roots may be used for decoration provided they do not help the turtle escape.

Cold frame: At the high end of the enclosure, in a place with plenty of sunshine, construct a cold frame with sheets of plexiglass. Even during lengthy spells of bad weather it will store enough heat because of the "greenhouse effect." Using a coping saw, you can easily cut a door-shaped opening in the glass to let the turtle in.

For extremely cold days when the temperature in the little house fails to reach about 79° F (26° C), install an infrared lamp, which can hang from the roof. Cement tiles are best for making the floor of the house.

My suggestion: The cold frame will also serve as a box in which your turtle can hibernate. Loosely filled with leaves and with more leaves heaped on top, it provides a frost-resistant resting place for the winter.

Feeding place: The turtle will graze on the grass and plants, but it will need additional food.

A fieldstone placed in front of the cold frame will serve as a "breakfast plate" and make it easy to remove leftovers from the enclosure afterwards.

Bathing facilities: At the low end of the enclosure, install a water basin with a spillway to allow easy runoff of rainwater; otherwise a cloudburst might force the turtle to learn to swim.

Well suited as swimming basins are the standard birdbaths made of cement or plastic that are found in gardening supply stores or pet stores.

Keeping Water Turtles Outdoors

Many marsh and water turtles are suited for staying outdoors in summer (see Popular Turtle Species, page 50).

Water volume: Roughly 79 gallons (300 L) of water, at least.

Enclosure: See the instructions for making an outdoor enclosure for land turtles.

Pond: Use a ready-made garden pond (available in specialty stores). Like the birdbath, it must have a drainage system that will protect the turtle from harm.

A large limb should protrude from the water (see illustration, page 19) so that the turtle can climb out of the water onto it. In the event of danger the turtle can simply drop into the water.

Important: A garden pond is not always suitable for turtles' hibernation. Winters in the northern parts of the United States, for example, are much longer than those in most of the turtles' homelands. After several winters outdoors the animals would die.

Plants: At most plant reeds and cattails. Everything else will be eaten, as will all fish and the larvae of salamanders and insects.

During the summer, give your turtle a chance to "fill up" on fresh air and sunshine in an outdoor pen. Cold frame (1) and birdbath (2).

Environment and Care

Bringing the Turtle Home

Dealers and breeders are experienced; they know how to pack your turtle for travel so it will suffer no harm. But for subsequent trips (vacation, trips to the veterinarian) it is useful to know how to transport your pet safely and carefully.

The turtle is safest in a cotton or cheesecloth sack. The fabric must be loosely woven and permeable to air, and the seam should be turned to the outside. Otherwise the animal can get tangled in the threads.

During the warm part of the year it is sufficient to put the bag holding the turtle into a box, with the animal's back up and abdomen down, of course. The bag should not be able to slide back and forth too much (see illustration, page 38).

During the cold part of the year put a hot-water bottle or heat-storing pillows on the bottom of the box, under the bag. Such pillows probably are more familiar to you as cold storage cells for transporting beverages. The temperature should not exceed about 79°F (26°C). Wrap the box in a small wool blanket or fill it with loosely crumpled newspaper.

Don't worry! The turtle will get enough air if you wrap or pack everything quite loosely, and it will be protected from cold drafts, which could prove fatal. Keep in mind that turtles, being poikilotherms, do not produce their own heat but must rely on an external source for their supply.

Once your pet returns home, it should have available a quarantine terrarium (see page 20) where it can spend the first few weeks.

Proper Acclimation

A newly acquired turtle must be housed at first in a quarantine terrarium (see page 20). When you buy a turtle you cannot tell by its appearance whether it is infested with worms or suffering from an amoebic infection. This will be determined only from stool samples (see page 22), which you can have examined in the office of your veterinarian.

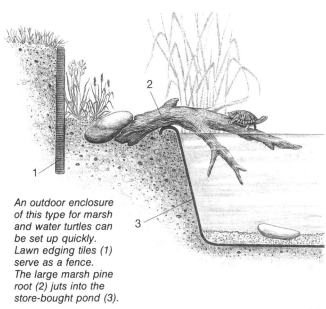

An outdoor enclosure of this type for marsh and water turtles can be set up quickly. Lawn edging tiles (1) serve as a fence. The large marsh pine root (2) juts into the store-bought pond (3).

Painted turtles live primarily in water. Quiet bodies of water full of plant growth are their na

Quarantine Is Indispensable

The turtle must remain in quarantine until it is "officially" pronounced to be in perfect health. Similarly, should illness occur later, care for the turtle in a quarantine terrarium, just to be on the safe side. In this way you can keep your pet from continuously spreading germs or worm eggs in the large terrarium and thus reinfecting itself right after its recovery.

The quarantine terrarium for land turtles measures about 24 × 20 × 20 inches (60 × 50 × 50 cm) and contains only those objects that are most expedient and easiest to keep clean (see illustration, page 23).

The quarantine terrarium for marsh turtles is equipped with a dish for bathing, whereas a water bowl suffices for the land turtle. However, you may also douse the marsh turtle with a flower sprinkler two or three times a day to keep its skin and shell pliant. In all other respects treat the animal as you would a land turtle in quarantine.

The quarantine terrarium for water turtles should measure 20 × 20 × 20 inches (50 × 50 × 50 cm). The only piece of equipment needed is a piece of ridge tile that serves the animal as a hiding place. Adjust the water level so that the back of the tile sticks out of the water to form an island.

Understanding body language is the key to a good relationship with your turtle. Without this knowledge you will scarcely be able to recognize the needs of your charge, much less fulfill them.

My suggestion: Water turtles often must be treated with powder or ointment. Then you can keep the animals for a period of hours or days in small cube-shaped pieces of dampened foam rubber or in peat moss (available in gardening supply stores). The skin and shell must not become dry. They should be sprinkled periodically.

First, a Bath

Before putting the turtle in quarantine, give it a thorough bath. While bathing your pet, check it thoroughly for injuries. Ticks or mites (see page 36) may have lodged themselves in the folds of its skin.

Land and marsh turtles should be placed in an ample bowl filled with warm water at a temperature of about 79°F (26°C). The turtle's head must be above water. During the bath, the animal can drink, and gradually any remaining pieces of dirt will be loosened from its body. As a rule, 10 to 20 minutes in the bath are enough.

The water turtle also needs to bathe before being placed in the quarantine terrarium so that its "swimming pool water" in the aquarium will stay clean longer.

After bathing the animal, put it in the quarantine terrarium or aquarium and let it first creep into its hiding place, where it can stay until it emerges voluntarily. You can speed up the process by offering the turtle fresh food daily.

How to Take Stool Samples

In the first few days after your turtle's arrival, take the initial stool samples. Many physicians and veterinarians have special containers with a small spoon attached to the lid. Any other receptacle with a lid that can be tightly closed will do just as well.

You need three containers because you will need to take samples on three consecutive days. A drop of water will keep the sample from becoming dry and losing its value. No harm is done if you have to wait longer for a sample. The first of the samples, however, should be no more than five days old when it reaches the veterinarian. Keep the samples in the refrigerator to prevent the growth of mold, which would make them unfit for use.

Important: Turtles excrete a whitish-yellow urine with a consistency ranging from viscous to crumbly. It has no value in determining whether or not your pet has parasites.

Getting Used to Other Animals

If the new turtle is to associate with another one already in your care, make sure that there is enough room for two in the hiding place and on the sunbathing island; otherwise there will be scuffles. Already-established animals will defend their territory—in this case, the entire terrarium—against newcomers, often quite fiercely. If this happens, the old, inhospitable animal has to be quarantined for two weeks. During this time the new turtle can explore the territory, gain confidence,

The time switch provides year-round control of heating and lighting.

Turtle Care at a Glance

How often	Land turtles and tortoises	Marsh turtles	Water turtles
Every day	Remove feces and urine; scrub water basin and fill with fresh water; feed.	Remove feces and urine; scrub and refill swimming basin; feed.	Change water of small aquariums; feed young turtles
Weekly			Change water of large aquariums; feed large animals two or three times
Every six months	Health check; stool sample	Health check; stool sample	Health check; stool sample

and become less easy to intimidate. If the fighting shows no signs of ending despite all your precautions, or if one animal does not dare to face the other one, refuses to eat, and stays in hiding, then each turtle will need its own terrarium.

The turtles may get along better in the outdoor enclosure in the summer. If they don't, wait until mating season (see page 39) to bring them together again. That ordinarily unites even the "grumpiest" partners—although not necessarily for any length of time.

Dogs, cats, guinea pigs, and mice should not come in contact with your turtle. Their curiosity and playfulness or the rodents' readiness to try their teeth on everything can have fatal results, especially for small turtles.

Why Turtles Need a Winter Rest Period

Turtles from temperate zones—that is, from Europe or the northern United States—need to spend the winter in a certain state of rest. The low temperature and lack of food make it impossible for these poikilothermic animals to survive in an active state. They manage by taking a so-called winter rest, a state in which all their bodily processes are slowed down immensely. All metabolic processes, the heartbeat, respiration, and movement are reduced to such an extent that the animals can easily make it through the brief winter in their homeland with small reserves of fat.

In the case of mature turtles the winter rest period also has a beneficial effect on reproductive behavior. In the long run hibernation is really necessary to preserve fertility.

"Turtle winters" in the northern United States, lasting from October until the end of March, are especially hard on small animals, which should not spend the entire time in hiberna-

tion. Three or four months are ample for full-grown turtles as well.

Hibernation does not take place if the turtle has a serious illness that must be completely cured. In this case

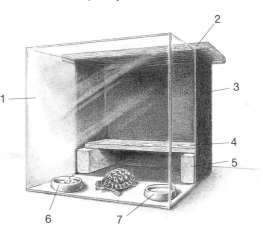

The quarantine terrarium for land turtles should not be decorated, just supplied with the essentials. Glass aquarium (1), board cover (2), black adhesive film (3), board (4), bricks (5), food dish (6), water dish (7).

omitting the winter rest period is not harmful. In the long run, however, it is stressful if the animal has no chance to reduce its reserves in winter and thus is forced to be active year after year without a break.

How to Recognize Readiness to Hibernate

Readiness to hibernate manifests itself in October, when there is a marked decrease in the length of the days and the intensity of the light. The turtle's activity falls off; it leaves its hiding place more infrequently and often stays with its head pushed into the darkest corner. Land and water turtles begin to lose their appetite or stop eating altogether.

Now it is time for you to get your pet ready for its winter rest.

Hibernation of Land Turtles and Tortoises

Observe the following rules:
- Bathe the turtle daily for two or three days—ten to twenty minutes each time—in water with a temperature of about 75 to 79°F (24–26°C) until it has completely emptied its intestine.
- Then turn off the heat and light in the terrarium and set the room temperature below 64°F (18°C). Leave it this way for two to three days.
- If this procedure reinforces the behavior described above, put the turtle in its hibernation box.

The young turtle will not be fully grown for another six to ten years.

- Weigh your pet beforehand. Smaller turtles may be weighed on letter scales. Check your pet's weight every five or six weeks during hibernation to make sure it is not suffering any harm. Keep in mind that a 10 percent weight loss during the winter rest period is normal for full-grown turtles, while young animals may lose as much as 15 percent.

The hibernation box should measure about 28 × 28 × 32 inches (70 × 70 × 80 cm). It consists of boards "casually" nailed together so that air may enter through cracks in the sides (see drawing, page 27). Fill the bottom of the box to a height of about 4 inches (10 cm) with damp (not wet) lava clinker or fired clay pellets (available in gardening supply stores). Layer peat moss that is almost dry but not withered, leaves, or bark chips on top of this up to a level about 4 inches (10 cm) from the rim of the box. Cover the box with cheesecloth or screen wire.

Room temperature: The hibernation box should be placed in a room where the temperature ranges from about 39 to 54°F (5–12°C).

Feeding: Do not feed the turtle during its winter rest period.

How Land Turtles and Tortoises Wake

After a winter rest of three or four months, bring the turtle out of its hibernation box and put it in its hideaway in the quarantine terrarium. For the time being it will continue to rest. Then move the terrarium to a room with a temperature of about 68 to 72°F (20–22°C) and wait for the turtle to emerge on its own. Several things need to be done now:
- Bathe the animal in warm water—about 75 to 79°F (24–26°C)—to which you have added one level teaspoon of table salt for each quart (L) of water.

Hurry across! Terrain that offers little cover makes turtles uneasy.

• When the turtle has drunk its fill, it can return to its terrarium. The heating and lighting should be set at the customary levels (see page 8).
• Offer your pet fresh food and water daily, even if it will not eat for the first week or so.
• Weigh the turtle to see whether it has lost more than 10 percent of its weight.

Hibernating in the Open

If your basement does not grow cold enough in winter to reach the required minimum temperature, it is always suitable for the turtle to winter outdoors.

The hibernation box in this case is sunk into the ground. For safety heap about 20 inches (0.5 m) of straw or leaves on top of the box and the immediate surroundings to keep severe frost away from the turtle. If there are rats on your property, protect the box with a cover of fine-mesh screen wire before you lower it into the ground.

Hibernating in the cold frame inside an outdoor enclosure (see page 16) is quite a comfortable matter. Fill the cold frame halfway, following the instructions given for the hibernation box, and put your pet inside. After a few days, once you are positive that it has dug itself in, cover the little house with leaves or straw. We use this method successfully in our zoo. Be-

Differences in Taking Care of Turtles

	Land turtles and tortoises	Marsh turtles	Water turtles
Type of accommodation	Earth terrarium (dry); in the yard an outdoor terrarium as well; possibly a hibernation box. Equipping the enclosure is simple; technical accessories are needed (see page 10).	Marsh terrarium; in the yard in outdoor terrarium with a swimming pool as well. Equipping the enclosure is demanding; technical accessories are needed (see page 11).	Aquarium; in the yard an outdoor terrarium with a pond as well; hibernation in aquarium; technical accessories are needed (see pp. 14–15).
Taking care of accommodations	Easy.	Easy, but change water often.	Costly, because large quantities of water must be changed.
Feeding	Chiefly plants; on land.	Chiefly meat; in the water or land.	Chiefly meat, in the water.
Most common mistake	Keeping animal on floor, with resulting eye and lung inflammation	Inadequate hygiene, resulting in infections and intestinal parasites.	Drafts and water that is too cold, resulting in eye and lung inflammation.

cause the floor of the little house is covered with stone slabs, hungry rats pose no threat.

Hibernation of Marsh and Water Turtles

Observe the following rules:
• A bath to evacuate the intestine is not necessary. Especially thorough evacuations in the autumn, however, are a sign that the turtle is striving to hibernate.
• Turn off the heat and lights; the filter and ventilation can stay on.
• Wait until the aquarium water has reached room temperature. Set the water temperature below 64°F (18°C) for a few days.

• If the turtle becomes increasingly motionless and its passive behavior intensifies, put it into the hibernation aquarium.
• Weigh the turtle beforehand, using a letter scale for smaller animals.

As a hibernation aquarium, use the quarantine basin described on page 20 or a plastic tub with a capacity of about 127 quarts (120 L). The water level should be at a height about 2 inches (5 cm) above the top of the turtle's carapace. A piece of ridge tile will serve as a hiding place. Ventilation and filtration are not necessary. If the water turns cloudy, replace it with fresh water at the same temperature.

The water temperature may range between about 39 and 54°F (4 and 12°C). Take care that it does not exceed 54°F (12°C).

Food is not to be given the turtle during hibernation under any circumstances.

How Marsh and Water Turtles Wake

After four months at most, bring your turtle's "water bed" into a room where the temperature is about 72°F (22°C), and let the water reach room temperature. Then put the turtle into the water and put the heating and lighting on a normal setting. After two to seven days, as the temperature rises, you will begin to see an increase in the turtle's activity level and willingness to eat.

Your pet's weight should be checked according to the instructions given for the land turtle.

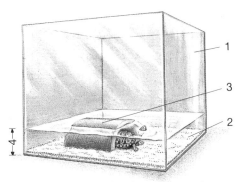

A hibernation aquarium for a water turtle should be equipped simply. Glass aquarium (1), layer of fine-grained sand (2), piece of ridge tile (3), water level (4).

Premature Waking from the Winter Rest Period

Usually this occurs when temperatures are unseasonably warm. You have two alternatives:

Wait it out: Wait a few days to see if the weather gets colder again. The turtle has about one week of "Built-in safety." During this time it grows slightly more alert, but it can drop rapidly back into its state of winter rest if temperatures drop. A colleague once told me how tough Mediterranean spur-tailed tortoises are. He keeps his turtles in an outdoor enclosure year-round. One of them dug itself in for its winter rest next to the roots of a bush. The root system kept it from getting in very deep, and its hindquarters were still protruding from the dirt. Checking on the animal from time to time, my friend found that its rear part was frozen solid.

When spring came, the turtle woke. It is still running around unharmed today.

Wake up the turtle: If the turtle continues to be restless, begin the standard "waking procedure."

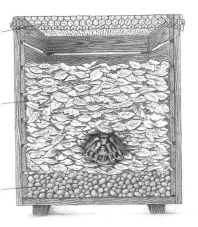

The land turtle can hibernate in this roomy wooden box. Expanded clay (1) is capable of storing moisture. On top of it put a layer of leaves, wood shavings, or peat moss (2). Cheesecloth or screen wire (3) make the best covers.

27

Diet and Feeding

If it were up to your turtle alone, its taste would dictate a diet consisting only of bananas and lettuce. This unbalanced diet, however, would damage the animal's health in the long run. Get your pet used to a healthful, varied diet without fail.

Mother Nature sets such a varied table for turtles that you will have a hard time approximating the richness of her offerings.

Vegetable Diet for Land Turtles and Tortoises

Grasses, weeds, and shrubs with many different kinds of leaves, flowers, and fruits grow in the turtle's natural habitat. On these plants are found insects, caterpillars, and snails, which provide the animal's small requirement of animal protein. Give free rein to your imagination and offer everything that meadow, garden, and vegetable market can provide: blossoms, fruits, seeds from meadow grass, herbs, and hay. Make sure the plants used for food are not poisonous and have not come into contact with herbicides or insecticides.

Turtles are very conservative eaters. Once they have accepted something as their main nutrient, they tend to favor it, sometimes to the exclusion of all other foods. You can solve this problem by adding finely chopped, nutritious supplements to their standard items. They will gradually grow accustomed to the taste.

The outdoor pen can also help your turtle out of this difficulty. Natural curiosity will lead it sooner or later to taste the numerous plants that grow there.

Important: In the final analysis, you should decide what your turtle eats. If the turtle's appetite were to be the determining factor, you soon would be offering an unbalanced diet of bananas and lettuce.

Meat Diet for Marsh and Water Turtles

Marsh and water turtles are omnivores; they eat a mixed diet that includes foods of both vegetables and animal origin. As a rule, they prefer a diet of meat, however.

Gather snails both with and without a shell (Watch out! The Roman, or edible, snail [*Helix pomatia*] is protected by the law on wildlife conservation and may not be gathered.), earthworms, grasshoppers, and other insects. You may use fat-free ground beef, but avoid pork altogether because of its high fat content. Small aquarium fish (guppies) or strips of fileted freshwater fish are also suitable. A highly nutritious basic food is dry cat food—any brand will do. Dry cat food is inexpensive and contains calcium, vitamins, and fish meat—precisely what marsh and water turtles need. In addition, pet stores offer an acceptable prepared food for marsh and water turtles.

A European pond turtle comes up for air. The water plants enrich its bill of fare.

Water turtles will eat only in water.

grow fat. Watch your pet while it eats and develop a feeling for when it should call a halt. Weigh the animal regularly to keep track of its weight increase, which in the first four to six years will start to slow down gradually (the growth in percentage terms decreases each year).

If your pet is so fat that its skin folds bulge like balloons when it tries to pull in its arms and legs, by all means reduce the amount of food.

Dietary Supplements

Only three additives—calcium, vitamins, and trace elements (available in pet stores)—should be given regularly, but they are crucial.

Calcium can be given in the form of crushed, pulverized eggshell, calcium carbonate, or a special preparation. Sprinkle it over the food of young turtles daily during the first two years; after that twice a week is sufficient.

Vitamins are administered in the form of drops or powder. Regardless of its age, a turtle needs one drop per day. Vitamin D3 is especially important for all turtles.

Trace elements are available in powdered form. Turtles of all ages need one pinch per week.

My suggestion: If you're wondering how to get the turtle to swallow all this, try the following:

Herbivores can be given the supplements in a little pureed banana at the beginning of their meal.

For primarily carnivorous turtles trickle the drops onto a piece of dry cat food. Powder can be mixed with a softened piece of dry cat food or with ground meat.

How Much Should Turtles Eat?

Unfortunately, there is no universally valid guideline for the correct amount of food. Healthy turtles often eat more than is good for them and

Feeding Water Turtles

When two turtles of different size live together, the larger animal can easily bite off the head of the smaller one if both try to eat the same piece of food simultaneously. Basically, land turtles should be fed on land from a flat dish, while water turtles need to eat in the water.

"Ambrosia" for Turtles

I want to share with you a special recipe from the kitchen of a successful turtle breeder. It will enable you to prepare a meal with any taste you choose for your turtle: you can offer your pet its favorite food and, at the same time, give it all the necessary additives (trace elements, vitamins, medicines if need be). Although this "ambrosia" is meant as a basis for feeding, it easily can serve as the sole diet during your vacation and thus make food preparation much easier for the substitute caretaker.

A Special Recipe

This recipe will enable you to keep readily on hand a food with high nutritious value.

Food for primarily herbivorous turtles consists of 85 to 90 percent vegetable matter, of as wide a variety as possible. The remaining 10 to 15 percent is fat-free ground beef.

Food for primarily carnivorous turtles is composed of up to 75 percent "meat," or rather, of animal protein, which may come also from squids, shrimp, liver, or chicken eggs. It is important to have a certain mix that you can also use on occasion to experiment with various tastes. Pork is excluded here as well. The remaining 25 percent of the preparation should consist of grass, weeds, or good hay.

Preparation is quite simple. First, wash all parts of the plants thoroughly. In a blender grind the plants with water to produce a pulp with the consistency of honey. Heat the mixture, stirring constantly (it burns easily), until a thermometer shows it has reached a temperature of about 175°F (80°C), and add the meat. Then add the following ingredients for each quart of the mixture: one level teaspoon of a mixture of mineral salts (trace elements) and one quarter of an effervescent vitamin tablet (that is high in vitamin D_3 and low in phosphorus), dissolved in water.

Continue to stir until the supplements are evenly distributed. Let the mixture cool to a temperature of about 140°F (60°C), and add powdered gelatin (available in grocery and health stores) according to the instructions on the package. Once the mixture has congealed, cut it into daily servings, which can be frozen in plastic bags and thawed as needed.

Basic Feeding Plan

Kind of food	Land turtles and tortoises	Marsh turtles	Water turtles
Plants	Meadow flowers, clover, wild and cultivated berries, fruit (not much banana), good hay.	Tender weeds, dark-leaf lettuce, fruit as a supplement, a few green peas. Do not use spinach!	Tender weeds, dark-leaf lettuce, fruit as a supplement, a few green peas. Do not use spinach!
Meat	A small grasshopper or the yolk of a hard-boiled egg or a comparable amount of fat-free ground beef once a week.	Dry cat food, fresh fat-free ground beef, slices of freshwater fish.	Dry cat food, fresh fat-free ground beef, slices of freshwater fish.
Supplements	Every two or three days one drop of a liquid multivitamin, a pinch of powdered vitamins (trace elements), and powdered calcium.	Every two or three days one drop of a liquid multivitamin, a pinch of powdered vitamins (trace elements), and powdered calcium.	Every two or three days one drop of a liquid multivitamin, a pinch of powdered vitamins (trace elements), and powdered calcium.

A buzzard uses the Galapagos giant tortoise—seen here in its natural habitat—as a landing field.

Five Rules for Feeding

1. Primarily herbivorous turtles are fed daily at the beginning of their active phase. Be sure that the food is always fresh, and replace any withered plants.

2. For full-grown plant eaters observe one fast day each week, giving them only hay.

3. Turtles that are primarily carnivorous should be fed twice a week.

4. Young carnivores (marsh and water turtles) need food daily, but in smaller quantities. So-called baby food is available in pet stores.

5. After the first or second year, feed young marsh and water turtles just as you would full-grown animals.

What to Do if the Turtle is Sick

An ounce of prevention is worth a pound of cure! This saying also holds true in the care of your turtle. The following preventive measure, which applies equally to all turtle species, must be observed without fail: never keep your turtle on the floor or window sill of your house. The drafts always present there—even though you may not notice them—have fatal consequences for turtles. The balconies of high-rise dwellings, too, are almost always drafty.

The following rule applies to all young turtles: provide a constant supply of calcium, vitamins, and ultraviolet light (see page 8).

Preventive Measures for Land Turtles

The swimming basin and the damp areas of sand that surround it are breeding grounds for abdominal and intestinal parasites and their eggs and larvae, as well as for amoebas and bacteria of all kinds. In the wild, turtles wander long distances and never again encounter the parasites they eliminate. In a terrarium, however, the situation is necessarily different. When the animals eat and drink, the germs they have eliminated are taken in once again. The germs renew their attack on the organism, and their number multiplies. The turtle, unable to cope, falls ill.

The most essential preventive measure, therefore, is this: scrub the water basin daily and keep the surrounding ground dry. Change the sand around the basin frequently (about every four to eight weeks, depending on how dirty it gets). Turtles like to deposit their feces in water. If this happens, change the water immediately.

Preventive Measures for Marsh Turtles

In respect to cleaning the water, take the same hygienic measures as those described for land turtles. Watch out for drafty air that may make its way through the opening of the terrarium. If the list of characteristics for a turtle (see Popular Turtles Species,

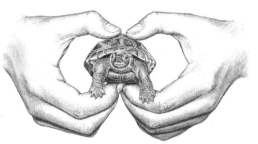

Testing the hardness of a young turtle's shell. A firm, undamaged shell is an indication that the animal is in good health.

page 50) specifies a water temperature of about 77 to 81°F (25–27°C), even indoor air with a temperature of about 70 to 75°F (21–23°C) can be relatively cold. Take precautions by reducing the size of the terrarium opening with panes of glass that partially cover it (see Terrarium for Marsh Turtles, page 11).

Preventive Measures for Water Turtles

Siphon off the feces immediately, unless it disperses rapidly in the water. If it sinks to the bottom, use a water hose to extract it.

If the excrement floats on the surface of the water, scoop it out with a cup, a fine-meshed tea sieve, or a paper coffee filter.

If your aquarium filter is well broken in, you can run the filter to collect widely dispersed feces.

If you keep a water turtle in warm water, a large part of the aquarium opening should be covered (see Preventive Measures for Marsh Turtles, page 33) to protect your pet from the drafts that could kill it.

Hooked bills that are too long must be shortened by the veterinarian.

Initial Symptoms

If you are in the habit of seeing to your turtle daily, you will notice any changes in your pet in plenty of time. If it becomes listless, stops eating for no apparent reason, and disappears into its hiding place for days on end, you need to consider whether the weather has turned cold suddenly or whether it is time for hibernation. If that is not the case, it is time to see a veterinarian.

Weigh your pet regularly, using letter scales for a relatively small animal. In this way you always have a means of checking on its weight to confirm your suspicions. If a young turtle is not gaining in the spring and summer or if a full-grown animal is not at least maintaining its weight, it is certainly time for an examination by a veterinarian.

My suggestion: Give yourself plenty of time to locate a veterinarian who knows something about turtles. Then, should the need arise, you are guaranteed that your turtle will receive help in plenty of time.

Frequently Occurring Illnesses

The following section lists common symptoms of illnesses.

Viscous, Foul-smelling Bowel Movements

Possible cause: An intestinal infection.

Treatment: Take several stool samples for the veterinarian and have them tested for salmonella, amoebas, and abdominal and intestinal worms. The veterinarian will prescribe the appropriate medicines. The animal should be quarantined until it is well. In the meantime, empty, scrub, and disinfect the terrarium. Disinfectants are available from your veterinarian or in pet stores.

Constipation

Possible cause: Too much dry food or too dry an environment. Does your pet have an opportunity to bathe daily? An amoebic infection in an advanced stage or a massive infestation of worms also can cause constipation.

Treatment: Your local veterinarian can provide a remedy.

Intestinal Prolapse

Symptoms: The intestine protrudes from the cloaca and is dragged along the ground. This problem should not

A parent and its young are seen together only in a terrarium. In the wild the parents do not involve themselves with the clutch of eggs, and the young are on their own as soon as they hatch.

Health Check

	Healthy turtle	Sick turtle
Eyes	Bright, no discharge	Dull, swollen, with small bubbles of mucus
Skin	Pliant, free of parasites	Dry, cracked, parasites in the folds
Shell	Firm, undamaged	Soft, distorted, injured
Anal region	Clean	Smeared with feces
Nose/mouth region	Dry	Small bubbles of mucus
Body shape	Evenly curved	Uneven, with dents or bumps
Behavior	Active, resists strongly when picked up	Apathetic, listless when picked up
Feces	Firm paste with no obtrusive odor	Viscous or liquid, foul-smelling

be confused with the swelling of the anal bladder or the penis in many water turtles. These conditions, unlike a prolapsed intestine, recede on their own after a few minutes. Intestinal prolapse in land and water turtles, however, persists for days.

Possible cause: Unclear; perhaps impairment of bowel function by foreign bodies.

Treatment: The turtle needs veterinary surgery immediately or it will die.

Swollen Eyelids

Possible cause: Drafts. In addition, water that is too cold and too dirty causes this reaction in water turtles.

Treatment: See a veterinarian at once and correct the condition that caused the illness. Be careful: if eye ointment is prescribed, apply it to the **undersurface** of the eyelid, not outside the lid.

Pneumonia

Symptoms: Noisy breathing, small bubbles at the mouth or nose.

Possible cause: Drafts or an environment that is too cold. In water turtles, listing while swimming is also a sign of lung inflammation.

Treatment: See the veterinarian at once, and change the turtle's environmental conditions.

Softening or Distortion of the Shell

Cause: Not enough calcium, vitamin D, and ultraviolet light.

Claws that are too long must be trimmed.

Treatment: If the deficiency is so acute that the shell already has softened, a change in your pet's diet will not help. Vitamin and calcium injections must be administered by a veterinarian if the animal is to be restored to health. Then you must prevent a recurrence by improving your pet's diet and giving it more ultraviolet light. Young turtles in particular need very attentive care in this respect.

Flaking of Shell and Peeling of Skin

These processes occur normally at regular intervals in all reptiles, leaving behind no bleeding or oozing wounds. If, however, you discover a sore on the animal's arms or legs after the flaking and peeling have ceased, some illness is present.

Possible cause: Infection caused by mites or fungus.

Treatment: See the veterinarian at once. Improved hygiene and periodic ultraviolet radiation will help prevent recurrences.

Injured or Fractured Shell

Cause: Accidents in which turtles fall to the hard floor from a great height (for example, from a table), are run over by their owner's car, or are bitten by a dog.

Treatment: See the veterinarian at once. If no organs are injured, the turtle has a good chance of survival even if the opening of the wound is so large that you can see inside its body. As a remedial measure provide your pet with a protected area for exercise, where such accidents cannot occur.

Bites and Superficial Wounds

Possible causes: Territorial battles or accidental injuries.

Treatment: If the lesions are so small that they stop bleeding on their own and hard scabs form within a few days, treatment by a veterinarian usu-

ally is unnecessary. To promote healing, you can bathe the areas with camomile tea or apply a healing ointment from your household medicine cabinet. Deep, gaping wounds or inflammations must be treated by a veterinarian.

Ectoparasites (Ticks and Mites)

In the skin folds, particularly those of the anal and neck areas, you occasionally will find a whitish, crumbly mass of dead skin beneath which large numbers of reddish dots are visible. These dots, no bigger than a pinpoint, are mites.

Ticks, as a rule, appear singly and are firmly lodged. Blackish brown in color, they range in shape from flat to round and are the size of a pinhead.

Treatment: The turtle must be quarantined and treated with medicine prescribed by a veterinarian. Often it is also possible to drip oil on the parasites, grasp them with special pincers (available in pet stores), and rotate carefully to remove them. If you are dealing with a tick infestation, the terrarium must be disinfected too.

Laying Distress

This term describes a state in which a female turtle has developed eggs but cannot lay them in the natural way.

Possible causes: Frequently the lack of a suitable place to deposit the eggs triggers this problem. Usually the bed of sand is too shallow. The absence of certain hormones also can lead to laying distress.

Treatment: If you notice that your turtle spends days digging a hole with its hind legs but does not lay any eggs, it may help to build up the ground. A height corresponding to the length of the shell should be adequate. However, if the turtle has a hormone deficiency, bring it to a veterinarian for an injection of oxytocin.

Excellent medicines are available for turtles, but the best medical attention is useless unless you observe the basic rules of care. Especially dangerous are the things a human does not "see," such as unsuitable temperatures, drafts, and inadequate terrarium hygiene.

An Indian roofed turtle with a little egret.

Routine Care

Although turtles may appear quite robust because of their "rough exterior," it is wise to check from time to time to see whether one of the following cosmetic procedures is necessary.

Overly Long Claws

Cause: Poor care. The turtle moves about too little and the ground is too soft; the animal has no way to keep its claws worn down.

Treatment: If need be, remedy matters by changing the ground material. For a quick fix trim the claws with nail clippers (see illustration, page 35). Some male water turtles, such as red-eared turtles, are an exception. The claws on their forefeet grow long naturally and should not be trimmed.

Overly Long Bill Edges

Cause: Too soft a diet.

Treatment: The horny edges of the bill must be filed down. As a preven-

During the cold season transport your turtle in a cardboard box. Put a hot-water bottle on the bottom and place the turtle, inside a cotton sack, on top of it.

tive measure, give your pet harder foods, including cuttlebone and limestone (available in pet stores).

Shell and Skin Care

Every two months rub your pet's skin and shell with vaseline: they will look ten years younger! Only don't use too much of a good thing. If the layer of petroleum jelly is too thick, it will clog the pores.

Turtles as Disease Carriers

Turtles under four inches in length may not be sold for pets. This law, administered by the Public Health Service, was enacted as an attempt to curtail the possibility of Salmonella transference from turtles to humans. Because of the manner in which they were kept and handled, many baby turtles host strains of Salmonella bacteria which can be passed on to humans. It was thought that the opportunity for transference was especially great if the turtle was small enough to be picked up by a toddler and placed in his/her mouth. Thus, the four inch rule came into being. However, the size of the turtle really doesn't matter if proper and adequate hygiene is not adhered to by the handler. *Always wash your hands and your child's hands before and after handling any turtle or tortoise.*

When Turtles Have Offspring

A pair of turtles will multiply "on their own" if the circumstances are right and if they have enough space. The "right circumstances" for European species are, above all, a winter rest period and a chance to live outdoors in summer.

Legal Regulations

Breeding protected turtle species is permitted but must be reported to the appropriate wildlife conservation authorities. The authorities can make the granting of the breeding permit contingent upon receipt of proof that the breeder is sufficiently knowledgeable and has appropriate accommodations.

Important: Turtles threatened with extinction (CITES I species) may not be bought or sold. This applies even if the animals are part of ranched populations. Ranched animals of the especially protected species (all CITES II species), however, may be marketed.

When Are Turtles Sexually Mature?

Turtles must be sexually mature before they can reproduce. European land turtles reach reproductive age between their third and fifth year, while European marsh turtles mature only between ten and twelve years of age. Many other species attain puberty between the ages of five and ten. However, the turtle's sexual maturity is not determined by age alone, but also by its growth rate and general living conditions.

The mating season of tropical and subtropical (subtropical refers to European or North American) turtles is determined by various outside

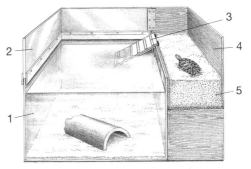

Water turtles also lay their eggs on land. Here's how you can make a place for your pet to deposit eggs. Aquarium (1), plexiglass attachment (2), gangway with aluminum brace (3), box for egg laying (4), sand (5).

influences. As a rule it occurs between the end of April and the end of May, brought about by the increase in the length of the days and the change in the position of the sun. Keeping turtles only under artificial light that does not vary in its duration has an inhibiting effect on the animals' readiness to reproduce.

Six Tips for Breeders

If you are reasonably certain that you have a male and a female of the

Before depositing her eggs, the female digs a pit where the eggs are laid one by one

right age, take good care of them, but they show no inclination to mate, you can stimulate their readiness to do so with a few tricks from breeders:

1. Separate the animals one or two months before you want them to mate, then reunite them at the proper time. In this case "separate" means put them beyond each other's range of vision, hearing, and smell, that is, at opposite ends of the yard. Alternatively, put one in a neighbor's yard. If you have arranged your pets' winter rest period so that they wake just at mating season, no further separation is necessary.

2. Three months before the mating season reduce the lighting time of the spotlight and terrarium lights to six hours per day. After two months, slowly increase the light exposure dur-ing the next three or four weeks to the "summer" maximum of ten to twelve hours.

3. At the same time change the temperature in the terrarium. Three months before the appointed time start to keep the water and air temperatures several degrees below the upper limits given previously. (For example, if the temperatures normally range from about 75 to 81°F [24–27°C], they now should not exceed approximately 72 to 73°F [22–23°C].) The heat source (the spotlight or the heating pad beneath) should not be turned on.

4. As you increase the light exposure, gradually turn up the temperature over a period of three or four weeks. During the last week turn on the spotlight and/or the heating pad

and then covered with dirt.

Young turtles dig themselves out of the ground on their own.

for a few hours at a time (see Housing Turtles Properly, page 8).

5. In the final week provide some "spring showers." Twice a day generously sprinkle the terrarium and the turtle with water, using a flower sprinkler. This will increase the humidity of the air in terrariums for land and marsh turtles. Higher humidity, along with rising temperatures, will stimulate the mating urge.

My suggestion: Use rainwater or decalcified water to sprinkle your pets. Otherwise, ugly calcium stains will be deposited on the sides of the terrarium over time.

6. Offer the animals fresh, tender foods. The turtles will hardly be able to ignore the coming of spring; they will start to engage in mating games and then proceed to mate.

Fertilization of the Eggs

If you're lucky and the turtles mate according to plan, you need to know what is happening inside your pets. The male produces sperm during the summer and stores them over the winter. The female also forms her ova in the summer and completes their development in spring, after the winter rest period. The eggs are fertilized before the shells are formed. Fertilization may take place even without the presence of a male, because many females can store spermatazoa for up to four years! Keep this in mind when buying a turtle. Even though your pet does not mate while in your care, it can lay fertilized eggs one to three years later.

Many newly hatched turtles still have a small yolk sac attached to their navel. It will shrivel and fall off if you keep the animal clean. If the tissue becomes inflamed, however, the turtle must be taken to a veterinarian.

The highlight of having a turtle in your care is successful breeding and raising of healthy young animals. As a rule, this is possible only if you have already gained some experience in caring for a full-grown turtle.

Reproduction of Land Turtles and Tortoises

Males affected by the mating urge are always on the lookout for a female. They make a beeline for anything that looks even remotely like a turtle of the same species and sniff at it. If it turns out to be a female of the same species—which is ascertained by the scent peculiar to each species—then the male circles the female. Sooner or later the female stops to watch her suitor, who now bites her on the forelegs, forcing her to draw in her head and legs. If the female also draws in her rear, the male encourages her by repeatedly butting her shell. In this way he tries to persuade her to move again so he can repeat the ritual described above. If the female finally decides to "play fair," the male mounts her from behind in order to copulate (see illustration, page 2). In so doing he utters hissing, whistling, or slightly "wheezing" sounds.

Reproduction of the Marsh Turtle

Many of the species that spend most of their time on land also court there, in much the same way as land turtles, but prefer to carry out the actual mating in the water. The ornate box turtle (see page 51) falls into this category.

Reproduction of the Water Turtle

The water turtle uses its swimming area for mating. Members of the genus *Chrysemys* swim toward the female from the front or from behind, shake their forelimbs near her head, and stroke her with their extremely long claws. Connected with this is a thorough preliminary investigation of the turtle's scent, which can be conducted even under water. Because the scent and the courtship rituals vary from species to species, making a mistake is out of the question. (The musk turtle, or stinkpot, got its name from its characteristic scent.)

In other species, after the sniffing ritual the male nods his head violently before trying to bite the female, which hides her head in her shell. Then the male seizes the edges of the female's shell with his claws in order to mate with her. In soft-shelled turtles this "foreplay" is much less pronounced.

Artificial Incubation of the Eggs

All turtle species bury their eggs on land, even when—like the soft-shelled turtle—they spend virtually all of their lives in the water.

Water turtles must be given an opportunity to leave the water so that they can bury their eggs in a box of sand. The box should be square and about twice as long as the turtle. It is best to place a box filled with sand next to the aquarium, so that the turtle can leave the water and climb onto it via a ramp. The sand should be as deep as the shell is long. Use appropriate attachments to prevent the female from climbing out at some other spot and falling (see illustration, page 39).

After the eggs have been deposited, pick them up—there may be six or more—and mark them on the upper side with a soft pencil. The eggs should not be turned during the entire incubation period, otherwise the embryo will be crushed by the yolk. A clear plastic box half filled with vermiculite—an insulating material used in the construction industry (if need be, simple building sand will do)—and with some water to moisten the insulating material will make a suitable incubator. Bury the eggs about halfway in the vermiculite (or sand). Close the transparent box with its lid. Inside the box the required 100-percent humidity will develop. Lift the lid once a day and swing it back and forth three or four times to fan fresh air into the incubator. Make sure the water condensed inside the lid does not drip onto the eggs. They could die if they become too wet. Put the box containing the eggs in a room with a temperature of about 81°F (27°C). This may be your furnace room, the cold frame in the outdoor enclosure, or an appropriately heated quarantine terrarium.

The young will hatch after 30 days (soft-shelled turtles); but it may take as long as 90 days (painted turtle) or 150 days (snake-necked turtle).

Raising the Young

Separate the hatchlings from their parents and raise them in another terrarium or aquarium. They need the same living conditions (temperature, food) as mature animals. Young turtles, however, do not eat immediately upon hatching. It takes about one week for their metabolism to switch from digesting yolk to digesting solid foods.

Cut the food in somewhat smaller pieces so the young animals can take hold of it easily. Make sure they have a regular supply of calcium and vitamins (see Feeding, page 28), but do not give megadoses of vitamins! That would be as harmful as too small a supply.

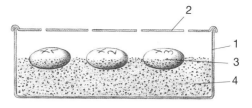

A clear plastic box (1), with a lid (2) that has air holes, serves as an incubator. The marked eggs (3) lie in a layer of building sand or vermiculite (4).

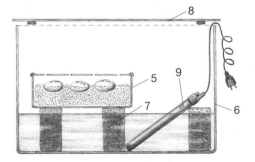

To control the air temperature in the incubator (5), place it on bricks (7) in a plastic aquarium (6) with a glass cover (8) that closes almost airtight. The heater (9), which has automatic control, ensures an even temperature for the incubation process.

Understanding Turtles

In the myths of many peoples turtles occupy a prominent place. According to an old Hindu legend, for example, the world was seen as a disc supported by four elephants. The four pachyderms were standing on the back of a huge turtle.

Turtles were already in existence at the time of the dinosaurs. Thus they belong to the few orders of the animal kingdom that have survived to the present day. The only others that have succeeded in doing so are lizards and crocodiles. The ancestors of the turtles alive today roamed the earth at a time when neither birds nor mammals existed, 180 million years ago.

Turtles in Myth and Legend

Among many peoples that live close to nature the turtle, as a part of the animate world, occupies a significant place. The Indians of North America saw the turtle as the creator of the earth's foundation. Originally, all the creatures lived on the back of a gigantic turtle that swam about in the ocean. When crabs brought sand from the ocean floor and heaped it on the turtle's shell, the earth as we know it was created and became habitable for humans and plants as well.

The Indians also hold the turtle in esteem as a friendly, sharp-witted counselor of infinite wisdom.

Body Language

Turtles do not make any noises, except in a few rare instances: during mating (see page 42) or when they are suffering from pneumonia (see page 35). Unlike cats and dogs, they cannot use their voice to express pleasure or pain. However, turtles do have their own body language, which they use to communicate with each other. If you're acquainted with the meaning of the individual behavior patterns, you can form some idea of what your turtle is trying to "say."

Pacing along or climbing on the wall: You frequently will see your pet ceaselessly roaming back and forth at the base of the terrarium wall, apparently searching for a way out of its cage. Or it may try continuously to climb over the upper edge of the enclosure at one of the corners. As a rule, these are clear signals that the animal is displeased with its living conditions. If the turtle has just moved into a new home, this behavior can be interpreted as curious exploration of its territory. If the efforts to escape do not decrease noticeably after three or four days, however, something is likely to be wrong with the terrarium climate. Strong odors or excessively loud noises also can impair the turtle's sense of well-being.

Digging in the ground: If your turtle digs in the ground unceasingly, it probably is a female trying to lay eggs but unable to find a suitable place to deposit them. It is also possible that your pet is looking for a hiding place or trying to hibernate (see page 23).

Burrowing in the gravel under water: Water turtles like to burrow in the gravel under water. Generally they are looking for food, but they may do so just to pass the time.

Stretched out on all fours: If the turtle is lying in the "sun" with its

From this position the water turtle surveys its surroundings with keen attention.

limbs outstretched and its head flat on the ground, it is basking and enjoying itself. However, if it lies in this position under the heat lamp **all day** and seems feeble, it may be seriously ill and in need of a veterinarian's care.

Raising its head: If the turtle gets up on all fours and cranes its neck, it is displaying a lively interest in its surroundings.

Pulling in its head and limbs: If your turtle withdraws its head and limbs all of a sudden, it is afraid and does not want to be disturbed.

Sensory Capacities of the Turtle

Smell: The turtle's excellent sense of smell leads it unerringly to its mate and its food.

Water turtles can smell under water just as well as on land. Thus they can reach their goal even in muddy water.

By moving the bottom of their mouth cavity, turtles pump water through their nose into their mouth and let it flow out of their mouth.

As much skin as possible is exposed when a turtle basks.

Sight: The turtle's keen eyesight enables it to spot food or enemies at a distance.

Thus the Mediterranean spur-tailed tortoise, for example, can recognize one of its favorite foods—yellow dandelion blossoms—from a great distance but not from close range. At close range it relies more on its sense of smell for orientation.

Hearing: A turtle's ears often are hard to see; they lie slightly behind the animal's "cheeks" and are often covered by leathery skin or scales.

There is no external auricle, so the eardrum lies just under the skin. Because turtles hear lower tones best, it is possible to speak to your turtle or to attract it with the low tones of an instrument. I know cases where turtles reacted to their owner's call or piano-playing and emerged from their hiding place to be fed.

Ground vibrations (footsteps, falling rocks) are transmitted via the legs and shell to the inner ear.

Turtle Anatomy

The shell: The most noticeable thing about a turtle is its shell. And the biggest mistake you could make would be to interpret this term literally. The shell is made up largely of living, vulnerable material.

The bony plates that form parts of the spine, ribs of the shoulder girdle, and ossified skin constitute the supporting structure. Thus the shell is part of the skeleton, which is covered by a sensitive periosteum. Anyone who has been kicked in the shin knows how sensitive this periosteum is. The periosteum on the turtle's shell is protected solely by the bony plates, or scutes. They are the only dead matter—comparable to the human fingernail.

Between the scutes, in the seams where light areas appear when growth is occurring, the periosteum is virtually unprotected. It is highly sensitive and should not be scratched, scrubbed, or probed with a fingernail!

The "growth rings" that are frequently observed provide information about the growth spurts of the shell, but are no basis for conclusions about the animal's age. Although the turtle's shell becomes somewhat uneven and thicker with age, it is also worn down from the outside as the animal roves about and rubs against roots, thorns, and rocks, and as it digs. As long as the animal is healthy entire scutes do not become detached, except in some species that live in the water (such as *Chrysemys, Cuora,* and *Chelodina*). In these species the outermost horny plate is sloughed off from time to time in a normal process. It then floats around in the aquarium, where it alarms concerned pet owners.

In soft-shelled turtles the shell develops in a special way. Actually, "retrogression" would be a better term for this process than "development," because the flat, bony arch of the carapace is covered only by a tough, leathery skin. The plastron consists of

Young turtles are lodged crosswise in the egg and often emerge from it sideways.

somewhat broader bones in the areas of the pelvis and shoulder girdle. Most of the plastron is covered only with soft skin.

It is astonishing, then, that a soft-shelled turtle buried in the sand "breathes" to a large extent through its skin; that is, it absorbs oxygen and gives off carbon dioxide. Partly for this reason the turtle is also highly sensitive to unclean water in the aquarium or to shell injuries.

Mediterranean spur-tailed tortoises.

The ornate box turtle has an additional peculiarity: hinged joints are "built into" its shell. This feature adds the finishing touch to the protection afforded by the shell in an amazing way. Normally—for example, in the case of the Mediterranean spur-tailed tortoise—the turtle retracts its head, arms, and legs into its shell while the coarse skin of the legs faces outward. The box turtle, however, can raise the front and rear portions of the plastron like a drawbridge. In this way it really "closes up shop" and is protected all around.

Other turtles mentioned in this book have similar mechanisms (the mud turtle [page 58] and the hingebacks with their hinged carapace [*Kinixys*, page 54]).

My suggestion: If someone offers you a turtle of the especially rare saw-back type—which has a symmetrically rounded shell—in all probability it is a deformed animal of another species suffering from rickets, which causes the individual bones and scutes to stand out singly like cones. I advise you not to purchase such an animal.

The color of the shell is subject to normal changes. Young painted turtles, for example, are as green as grass, while full-grown animals have a blackish-brown shell. Darkening of the shell, though less pronounced than in painted turtles, occurs in many other species as they age. Turtles living in captivity almost always have a more uniform color than animals of the same size that live in the wild. The latter usually have a brighter, more intense color, attributable to the sunlight, food, and natural "shell polish" available to them.

"Bill" and claws: Another conspicuous characteristic of turtles is their lack of teeth. In place of a row of white reptilian teeth, turtles possess jaws with sharp, horny edges that they use to chop plants to bits and to cut up meat.

Because the jaws are very powerful, the turtle can also bite a human hard enough to draw blood. Many species (such as soft-shelled turtles) can even inflict serious injuries and must be handled with particular care.

The horny edges can be curved toward each other at the tip to form a hook that can be used to secure the turtle's prey. In some species only the tip of the upper jaw is elongated (to assist in climbing). In the species described in this book, however, elongation of the bill, or tip of the upper jaw, is an abnormal development that requires correction (see illustration, page 34). Excessively long horny edges on the bill interfere with the turtle's ingestion of food.

A margined Mediterranean spur-thighed tortoise.

An eroded, or rosy, hingeback.

Just like the razor-sharp horny edges, the claws on the turtle's feet also continue to grow. Make sure your pet has an opportunity to wear down its claws in a natural way (see illustration, page 35). A turtle whose claws are too long can get stuck in cracks and tear its nails from their bed. Such an injury could result in serious inflammation.

Popular Turtles and Tortoises

In this guide I have described primarily those turtle species that are sold most frequently in pet stores. Turtles that are subject to CITES con-

The flared posterior margin of the shell is characteristic of the margined Mediterranean spur-thighed tortoise.

trols, European Community regulations, or the Federal Species Conservation Act are designated by the symbol Ⓢ (see What You Need to Know about Species Conservation, page 7). Moreover, you will find instructions for caring for strictly protected species that no longer may be bought or sold (see Important Information on Protected Turtle Species, page 60). They have been included in the guide because there are still private owners who have such turtles in their care.

Under the heading "Environment" I have provided, along with instructions on care, information on the temperature at which each species should be kept. These figures are only approximations. Please check an atlas of climate maps for additional information about the daily and annual fluctuations

in the temperature and humidity of your turtle's natural habitat. Using these data in combination with the information on geographic distribution, or range, given in the description of each species, you can easily vary the temperatures. The data on food in the instructions for care merely indicate whether a particular animal prefers plants or meat. Please read the chapter on diet and feeding, beginning on page 28, for more on this subject.

Land Turtles

Mediterranean Spur-tailed or Hermann's Tortoise Ⓢ

Testudo hermanni
Photo, page 48.
Size: Up to about 8 inches (20 cm).
Distribution: Greece and the Balkans as far north as the Danube. The subspecies *Testudo hermanni hermanni* lives in southern Italy, Greece, Albania, and Bulgaria. A second subspecies, *Testudo hermanni robertmertensi,* occurs in west-central and northwestern Italy, the Balearic islands, Corsica, Sardinia, southern France, and northeastern Spain.
Natural habitat: Open, steppelike land with scattered rocks and light patches of bushes; much sunlight and areas of light shade.
Environment: Terrarium and outdoor run enclosure; average air temperature from about 64°F (18°C) at night to 79°F (26°C) in the daytime. In the summer keep your pet outdoors as

often as possible, but only if a cold frame (see page 7) is available for cold nights (below about 61°F [16°C]) and the turtle can spend at least two or three daytime hours on stones with a temperature between about 90° and 97°F (32–36°C). A spotlight can be used to mimic sunlight (see page 8). In spring and fall the temperatures given above should be attained in the terrarium.
Behavior: Active in the daytime; likes to climb and dig; very lively if properly cared for.
Food: Plants.
Hibernation: Yes.
Species requiring similar care: Mediterranean spur-thighed tortoise, margined Mediterranean spur-thighed tortoise, Horsfield's tortoise.

Mediterranean Spur-thighed or Moorish Tortoise Ⓢ

Testudo graeca
Photo, page 52, **4.**
Size: May exceed 12 inches (30 cm).
Distribution: Southern Europe, Iran, Egypt, Libya, and Morocco. All four subspecies need the same care.
Natural habitat: See entry for Mediterranean spur-tailed tortoise.
Environment: See entry for Mediterranean spur-tailed tortoise.
Behavior: See entry for Mediterranean spur-tailed tortoise.
Food: Plants.
Hibernation: Yes.

Margined Mediterranean Spur-thighed Tortoise Ⓢ

Testudo marginata
Photo, page 52, **1.**
Size: About 12 inches (30 cm); the largest member of the genus.
Distribution: Southern Greece (this species is the true "Greek" tortoise); also has been introduced into Sardinia and Italy.
Natural habitat: Sunny slopes with a dense growth of grass and bushes through which the turtle tramples narrow paths.
Environment: See entry for Mediterranean spur-tailed tortoise.
Behavior: See entry for Mediterranean spur-tailed tortoise.
Food: Plants.
Hibernation: Yes.

Horsfield's or Afghan Tortoise Ⓢ

Testudo horsfieldii
Photo, page 52, **1.**
Size: Up to 8 inches (20 cm).
Distribution: Northeast of the Caspian Sea and from eastern Iran to Pakistan, in deserts and mountains (at altitudes of 5,000 to 7,000 feet). Dry sand and loamy soil; scattered patches of grass and bushes.
Natural habitat: See entry for Mediterranean spur-tailed tortoise.
Environment: See entry for Mediterranean spur-tailed tortoise.
Behavior: See entry for Mediterranean spur-tailed tortoise.
Food: Plants, especially flowers and fruits; rarely eats grass.
Hibernation: Yes.
Special features: This species digs underground burrows up to 36 feet (12 m) in length. The outdoor terrarium should be constructed so as to prevent your pet from breaking out underground as well. It needs an additional "dry period" of dormancy in summer, when it will eat very little and rest in its hiding place. Eight months may pass between egg laying and the hatching of the young.

Eastern Box Turtle Ⓢ

Terrapene carolina
Photo, page 52, **2.**
Size: Up to about 6 inches (15 cm).
Distribution: Eastern USA
Natural habitat: Open woodlands, damp meadows, stream edges; often encountered in areas of rich soil

Mediterranean spur-tailed tortoises (above), in contrast to Mediterranean spur-thighed tortoises (below), have a divided shell above the base of the tail.

1 *Horsfield's tortoise.*

3 *Red-footed tortoise.*

4 *Mediterranean spur-thighed tortoise.*

2 *Eastern box turtle.*

5 *Bell's hingeback tortoise.*

Whether you decide to keep a land or a water turtle, you must always comply with the requirements of the species in question. Only in this way will you find lasting pleasure in your pet.

ed-eared turtle.

uropean pond turtle.

8 *Painted turtle.*

and sandy, semiarid soil with light brush and nearby bodies of water.
Environment: Terrarium and outdoor enclosure; air temperature between about 64°F (18°C) at night and 82°F (28°C) during the day. Morning and evening "sunlight" in the terrarium.
Behavior: Active at twilight (morning and evening); spends the day in hiding.

Reeves' turtle.

Food: Meat, canned dog food, worms, snails. Supplement the diet with plants, including mushrooms.
Hibernation: Yes.
Special features: A hinge running horizontally across the plastron allows this turtle to "tuck itself up" by drawing up the segments. It can eat poisonous mushrooms without being harmed. This species is recommended only for those experienced in taking care of turtles.

Bell's Hingeback Tortoise Ⓢ
Kinixys belliana
Photo, page 52, **5.**
Size: About 8 inches (20 cm).
Distribution: Central and southern Africa, Madagascar.
Natural habitat: Steppelike land with sandy, gravelly soil; dry; scattered patches of grass and bushes.

Environment: Terrarium and outdoor enclosure; air temperature ranging from about 68°F (20°C) at night to 86°F (30°C) in the daytime. In the outdoor pen only during hot summer weather; in the terrarium on cooler, cloudy days.
Behavior: Active during the day.
Hibernation: No.
Special features: Rear hinge set into the carapace so as to give the hindquarters full protection.

Species requiring similar care:
Home's hingeback S, *Kinixys homeana;* size, about 8 inches (20 cm); inhabits the tropical rain forests of western Africa. Needs higher humidity (70–90 percent relative humidity) and higher air temperature: from 75°F (24°C) at night to 86°F (30°C) in the daytime.
Eroded hingeback S, *Kinixys erosa,* (see photo, page 49); size, up to 12 inches (30 cm) (the largest species of the genus); lives in the tropical rain forests, marshes, and shady river banks of western Africa. Needs higher humidity level and air temperature: see entry for Home's hingeback.
Red-footed tortoise S, *Testudo* or *Geochelone carbonaria* (see photo, page 52, **3**); size, up to 20 inches (50 cm); lives in tropical rain forests of South America. Needs higher humidity level and air temperature: see entry for Home's hingeback.
Tip: It is very difficult for a beginner to create the climatic conditions of a tropical rain forest in an aquarium.

Water and Marsh Turtles

Red-eared Turtle Ⓢ
Chrysemys [Pseudemys] scripta elegans
Photo, page 53, **6.**
Size: Up to 10 inches (25 cm).
Distribution: USA east and west of the Mississippi.

Natural habitat: Still, weed-filled waters that warm up quickly in the sun.

Environment: Aquarium and garden pond; aquarium water temperature between 79 and 82°F (26–28°C) and air temperature between 79 and 90°F (26–32°C). May be kept outdoors from June to August or September provided that a body temperature of about 97°F (36°C) is maintained for at least three or four hours per day in the sun, outside the water, and provided that the weather grows no colder than about 72°F (22°C).

Behavior: Active during the day; likes to bask in a spot just above water level; vigorous swimmer.

Food: The young eat meat, but as they age these turtles increasingly prefer plants.

Hibernation: Yes, but no longer than ten to twelve weeks.

Special features: Keeping a single turtle is preferable if there are no plans for breeding. Somewhat cantankerous if the living quarters are cramped.

Species requiring similar care:
Cumberland turtle, *Chrysemys (Pseudemys) scripta troosti;* size, up to 10 inches (25 cm);
River cooter or hieroglyphic turtle, *Chrysemys (Pseudemys) concinna hieroglyphica;* size, up to about 16 inches (40 cm).

Stinkpot, Stinking Jim, or Common Musk Turtle

Sternotherus odoratus
Photo, page 56, **10.**
Size: Up to 6 inches (15 cm).
Distribution: USA to southern Canada.
Natural habitat: Still, weed-filled bodies of water with flat banks.
Environment: Water terrarium and garden pond. Animals from the north-

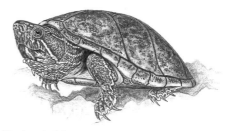

The head of the common musk turtle, or stinkpot, has a characteristic shape.

ern USA need a water temperature ranging from 68 to 77°F (20–25°C), while those from the southern states require temperatures between 73 and 82°F (23–28°C); air temperature: 75 to 82°F (24–28°C).

Behavior: Active in the daytime and at night; great eaters.
Food: Primarily meat.
Hibernation: Yes and no, depending on your pet's place of origin. If in doubt, careful observation of the animal in the fall (see page 23) can help you decide.
Special features: If the turtle is annoyed it secretes a strong-smelling fluid. Because this turtle is a poor swimmer, it needs an area of shallow water where it can rest touching the bottom.

Species requiring similar care:
Black Caspian turtle S, *Clemmys* (or *Mauremys*) *caspica rivulata;* size, up to 8 inches (20 cm). At home in lakes and rivers; eats meat; need for hibernation should be determined by behavior.

9 Spanish turtle.

10 Stinkpot or common musk turtle.

Turtles that need to rest in winter should be allowed to do so. Their vital rhythm depends entirely on observing a period of hibernation. You probably can imagine how your busy life would look if you never were allowed to take a vacation and truly relax. The turtle would fare the same without its winter period of dormancy.

11 Malayan box turtle.

56

Yellow-margined box turtle.

Spotted turtle.

Black marsh turtle.

15 Snake-necked turtle.

16 Mississippi map turtle.

European pond turtle S, *Emys orbicularis* (see photo, page 53, **7**); size, up to 6 inches (15 cm). Lives in marshy regions of Europe; eats meat; must hibernate.

Mississippi Map Turtle
Graptemys kohnii
Photo, page 57, **16**.
Size: Up to 10 inches (25 cm).
Distribution: Southern USA.
Natural habitat: Small, quiet bodies of water, warm and full of weeds, insects, and fish.
Environment: Aquarium with a sunbathing island, or garden pond; water temperature, 72–82°F (22–28°C); air temperature, 72–82°F (22–28°C). The basking platform above the water is especially important. Use an outdoor enclosure only on really hot summer days when your pet's body temperature can attain 97°F (36°C).
Behavior: Active in the daytime.
Food: Eats plants and supplements its diet with meat to a greater degree than usual.
Hibernation: Yes.

Species requiring similar care:
Spanish turtle S, *Clemmys caspica leprosa* (see photo, page 56, **9**); size, up to 10 inches (25 cm). Lives in rivers in Spain, Portugal, and Algeria. Observation will tell whether your turtle needs to hibernate.
False map turtle, *Graptemys pseudographica;* size, up to 10 inches (25 cm). There are four subspecies, which live in bodies of water with rich vegetation. They eat plants and supplement their diet with a great deal of meat. Hibernation is recommended.
Caspian turtle S, *Clemmys* (or *Mauremys*) *caspica caspica;* size, up to 10 inches (25 cm). There are three subspecies, which live in slow-running waters south of the Caspian Sea. They eat a diet of plants supple-

M ost turtles that live in the water like to swim extensively. For this reason you need a large aquarium that can provide these species with a large enough area for swimming.

mented with a great deal of meat. Observation will tell whether your turtle needs to hibernate.

Spotted Turtle
Clemmys guttata
Photo, page 57, **13**.
Size: Up to 5 inches (12 cm).
Distribution: In the eastern and northeastern USA, from Florida to Michigan and Ontario.
Natural habitat: Small, marshy bodies of water in meadows and slow-flowing rivers; bodies of water in swamplands.
Environment: Aquarium and outdoor enclosure; water temperature, 72–81°F (22–27°C); air temperature, 72–82°F (22–28°C). In the outdoor pen only on hot summer days when your pet's body temperature can reach about 97°F (36°C) out of the water.
Behavior: Active during the day; spends a great deal of time submerged if the water is warm enough; if the water is cool it suns itself frequently.
Food: Plants and meat (in the wild they are mostly carnivorous).
Hibernation: Yes.
Special features: The males have brown eyes, the females, yellow. In calculating the length of the hibernation period, remember that the species is dispersed over a wide area from north to south. Hence the animals may be accustomed to periods of dormancy that vary greatly in length.

Reeves' Turtle
Chinemys reevesii
Illustration, page 54.
Size: Up to 7 inches (17 cm).
Distribution: Indonesia, Japan, Korea, and especially southeastern China.
Natural Habitat: Quiet bodies of fresh or brackish water.
Environment: Aquarium and outdoor

enclosure. The aquarium should be arranged so that this turtle, a poor swimmer, can crawl from beneath the water to the surface. In the outdoor pen only on hot summer days when the water reaches a temperature of 81°F (27°C), because the species on the European market originate in the southern portion of the animals' geographical range. Water temperature, about 75 to 81°F (24–27°C); air temperature, about 75 to 82°F (24–28°C).
Behavior: Active during the day.
Food: Primarily meat.
Hibernation: No.

Species requiring similar care:
Indian roofed turtle, *Kachuga smithii* (see photo, page 37). Lives in the Indus and western Ganges rivers (is a rapid swimmer), eats primarily plants; does not hibernate.
Snake-eating box turtle, *Cuora flavomarginata* (see photo, page 56, **11**). Originates in southern China and Taiwan.

Common Mud Turtle
Kinosternon subrubrum
Size: Up to 5 inches (12 cm).
Distribution: USA on the eastern seaboard and the flatlands along the Mississippi and its tributaries.

Natural habitat: Quiet, shallow waters rich in vegetation.

Environment: Water terrarium and outdoor enclosure. The water terrarium should be one-half land and one-half water, with a flat bank that can be climbed easily. This turtle is a poor swimmer and spends a lot of time on land. The outdoor pen can be used from late May to September. Water temperature, 73 to 75°F (23–24°C); air temperature, 72 to 82°F (22–28°C).
Behavior: Active in the morning and evening; inactive during the remainder of the day and at night. Because it is aggressive toward members of the

same species, I recommend that novices keep only one turtle.
Food: Young animals: 50 percent water insects and 50 percent plants; growing animals: plants and meat in equal proportions.
Hibernation: Yes and no, depending on geographic origin. Use your pet's

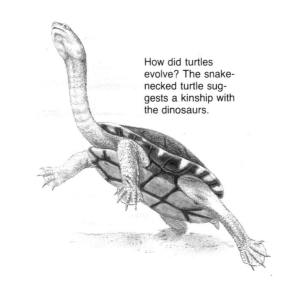

How did turtles evolve? The snake-necked turtle suggests a kinship with the dinosaurs.

behavior as an indicator of its need for a dormant period (see page 23).
Special features: A hinged plastron enables this turtle to close off the openings in its shell. It may secrete a strong-smelling liquid. The male's tail ends in an extremely horny tail.

Malayan Box Turtle
Cuora amboinensis
Photo, page 56, **11.**
Size: Up to 8 inches (20 cm).

Distribution: Southeastern Asia.
Natural habitat: Quiet, still bodies of water.

Environment: Aquarium with underwater climbing aids to help this turtle, a poor swimmer, reach the surface. Water temperature, 75 to 86°F (24–

30°C); air temperature, about 79 to 86°F (26–30°C).

Important: If the temperature drops below 64°F (18°C) even for a short time, the turtle's health may suffer.

Behavior: Active during the day.

Food: Meat and plants. The species is rather voracious.

Hibernation: No.

Black Marsh Turtle

Siebenrockiella crassicollis
Photo, page 57, **14**.

Size: May exceed 15 inches (38 cm).

Distribution: Southeastern Asia in tropical rain forests and savannas.

Natural habitat: Marshy pools, ponds, and bodies of running water of all kinds.

Environment: Aquarium with underwater climbing aids; water and air temperature between 75 and 86°F (24–30°C).

Behavior: Active during the day; calm disposition.

Food: Meat and plants in approximately equal proportions.

Hibernation: No.

Snake-necked Turtle

Chelodina longicollis
Photo, page 57, **15**.

Size: Up to 12 inches (30 cm).

Distribution: Eastern Australia.

Natural habitat: Quiet, slow-moving bodies of water and shallow banks. Also on land in rainy season.

Environment: Fairly large aquarium; water temperature, 73 to 82°F (23–28°C); air temperature, 75 to 82°F (24–28°C).

Behavior: Active during the day; vigorous swimmer; quite vicious in mating season.

Food: Meat (aquatic insects, tadpoles, frogs, and fish).

Hibernation: No.

Special features: This turtle protects its head and neck by moving them to the side, between the carapace and plastron (suborder *pleurodira*, meaning side-necked).

Painted Turtle

Chrysemys picta
Photo, page 53, **8**.

Size: Up to 10 inches (25 cm).

Distribution: USA east of the Mississippi and in the northern part of the country west of the Mississippi.

Natural habitat: Quiet, weed-filled bodies of water.

Environment: Aquarium and outdoor enclosure; water temperature, 68 to 77°F (20–25°C); air temperature, 68 to 77°F (20–25°C). In the aquarium place a spotlight above the turtle's "island" to offset the low water temperature. Use the outdoor pen from late May to September.

Behavior: Active during the day; alternates constantly between looking for food and basking in the sun.

Food: Meat and plants in equal parts.

Hibernation: Yes.

Important Information on Protected Turtle Species

On page 7 of this guide, you will find the essential information on the subject of species conservation. The material below will give you a good general idea which of the popular turtle species described in the section beginning on page 50 are protected by CITES and by European Community regulations.

Land Turtles

Mediterranean spur-tailed tortoise:

Listed in Appendix II of CITES. Also protected under Annex C1 of the European Community law, which augments CITES.

Mediterranean spur-thighed tortoise: See entry for Mediterranean Spur-tailed tortoise.

Margined Mediterranean spur-thighed tortoise: See entry for Mediterranean Spur-tailed tortoise.

Horsfield's tortoise: Listed in Appendix II of CITES.

Eastern ornate box turtle: All box turtles are listed in Appendix II of CITES.

West African hingeback: Listed in Appendix II of CITES. In addition, protected by the European Community decree, Annex C2. This means that Europe requires an import license for this turtle species.

Home's hingeback: See entry for West African hingeback.

Eroded hingeback: See entry for West African hingeback.

Red-footed turtle: See entry for West African hingeback.

Turtles That Live in the Water/Marsh Turtles

Red-eared turtle: Listed in Appendix II of CITES.

Because the present regulations are subject to continuous review and must conform with the most recent data on the actual numbers of each turtle species in existence, you should, if the need arises, write to:
Division of Law Enforcement
Fish and Wildlife Service
U.S. Department of the Interior
Washington, DC 20240

Index

Boldface numbers indicate color photos. C = cover.

ADDRESSES AND BIBLIOGRAPHY

American Federation of Herpetoculturists
P.O. Box 1131
Lakeside, CA 92040
(International reptile and amphibian organization. Publish
    "The Vivarium" magazine)

Pet Information Bureau
c/o Tina Carroll
111 Fifth Ave.
New York, NY 10003
Phone: 212-4200-8100 or 800-223-2121

Books

Alderton, D., 1987. *Turtles and Tortoise of the World.*
    Aqua Stock/Petcetera; Bayonne, NJ.
Frye, F. L., 1973. *Husbandry, Medicine and Surgery in*
    Captive Reptiles. V. M. Publishing, Inc.; Bonner
    Springs, Kansas.

Cover photos:

Front cover: A Mediterranean spur-tailed tortoise.
Inside front cover: Hieroglyphnic river cooter and two red-eared sliders.
Inside back cover: Caspian turtles basking in the sun.
Back cover: Red-eared slider.

Photographers:

Angermeier: p. 32; Cram/Silvestris: p. 49 *top*; G. Denzau-Neumann: p. 37; Jacana: pp. 12 *left*, 16, 17, 52 *center right*, 57 *top right*; Kahl: *inside front cover,* pp. 52 *bottom right*, 52 *top left and bottom left*; Lankinen/Transglobe Agency: pp. 20/21; Limbrunner: pp. 40, 41; Layer: pp. 25, 53 *bottom left, inside back cover*; Pforr: pp. 9, 12/13 *center right*, 25; Reinhard: pp. 48, 49 *bottom,* 52 *top left and bottom right,* 53 *top,* 56 *center left and bottom right*; Rohdich: pp. 29, 45; Thomsen/Transglobe Agency: pp. 41 *right,* 53 *bottom right*; Wothe: pp. 5, 24.

Important information:

Keep in mind the hazards associated with the use of electrical appliances and wiring, especially near water. I strongly urge that you buy an electronic circuit breaker that will interrupt the supply of electricity if there is some breakdown in the appliances or lines. A protective switch which must be installed only by an expert works in the same way.

Inside front cover: *Many turtle species, like these three red-eared turtles, are brightly colored only when young.*

636.5   12720

WIL TURTLES: A
COMPLETE PET OWNER'S
MANUEL — H. Wilke

DATE DUE			

2/15 $5.95